AUTOMOTIVE
IN ART
by
Shan Peck

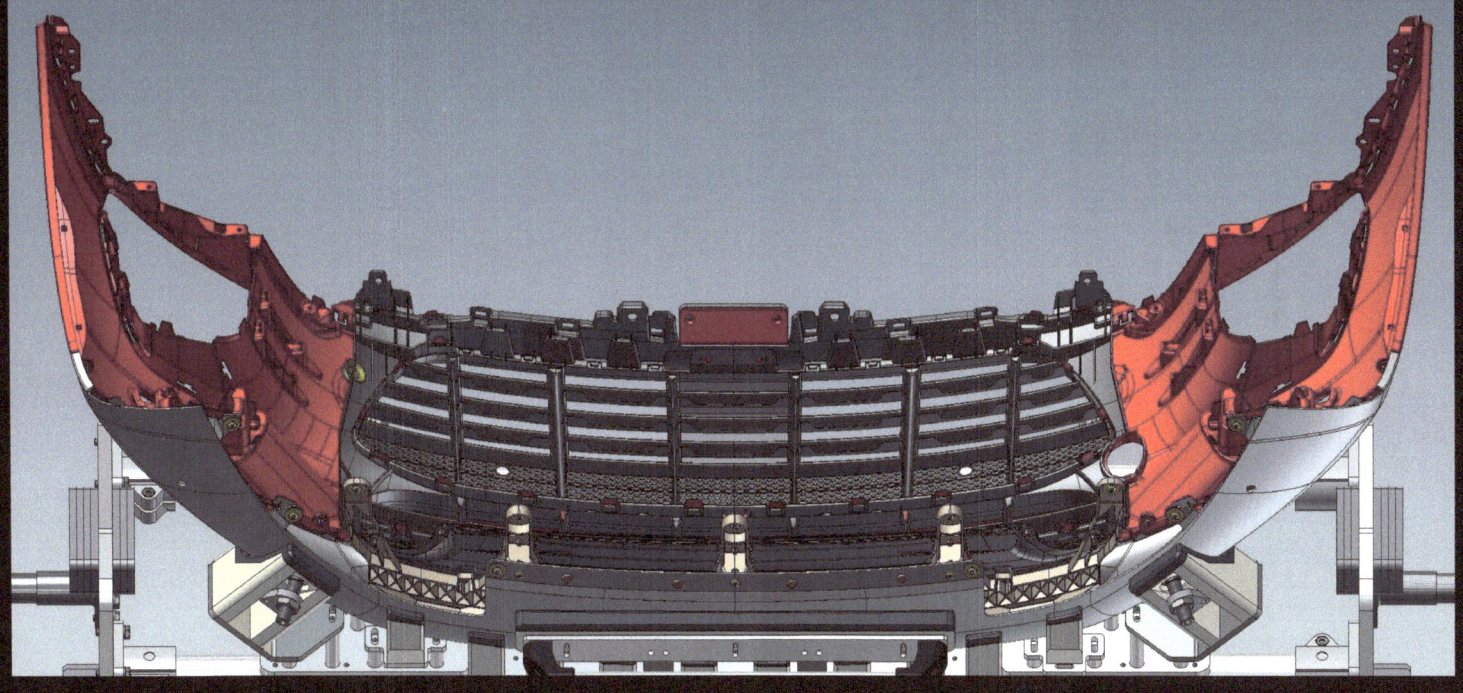

Shan Peck has asserted his right under the Copyright, Design and Patent Act 1988 to be identified as the author of this work. This book is the work of creative artists and, except in the case of historical fact, any resemblance to actual persons, not specifically named in the book, living or dead, is purely coincidental. Every effort has been made to obtain the necessary permissions concerning copyright material, both illustrative and quoted. We apologize for any omissions in this respect and will be pleased to make the appropriate acknowledgments in any future edition.

First published in United States of America in 2021.

Book design by Shan Peck.
Front cover page artwork by Lance Wurst, Ron Patterson and David King.
Rear cover page artwork by David King and Ron Patterson. Photography by authors daughter Lucia.

Copyright © 2021 Shan Peck
All rights reserved
ISBN: 9798482450826

DEDICATION

I would like to dedicate this book to all those artists I had the privilege to get to know since 2015 and to all those who trusted me with their art and participated in my art books.

Featured Artists

Lance Wurst

David King

Ron Petterson

Shan Peck

Yellow 1953 Buick by David King Studio

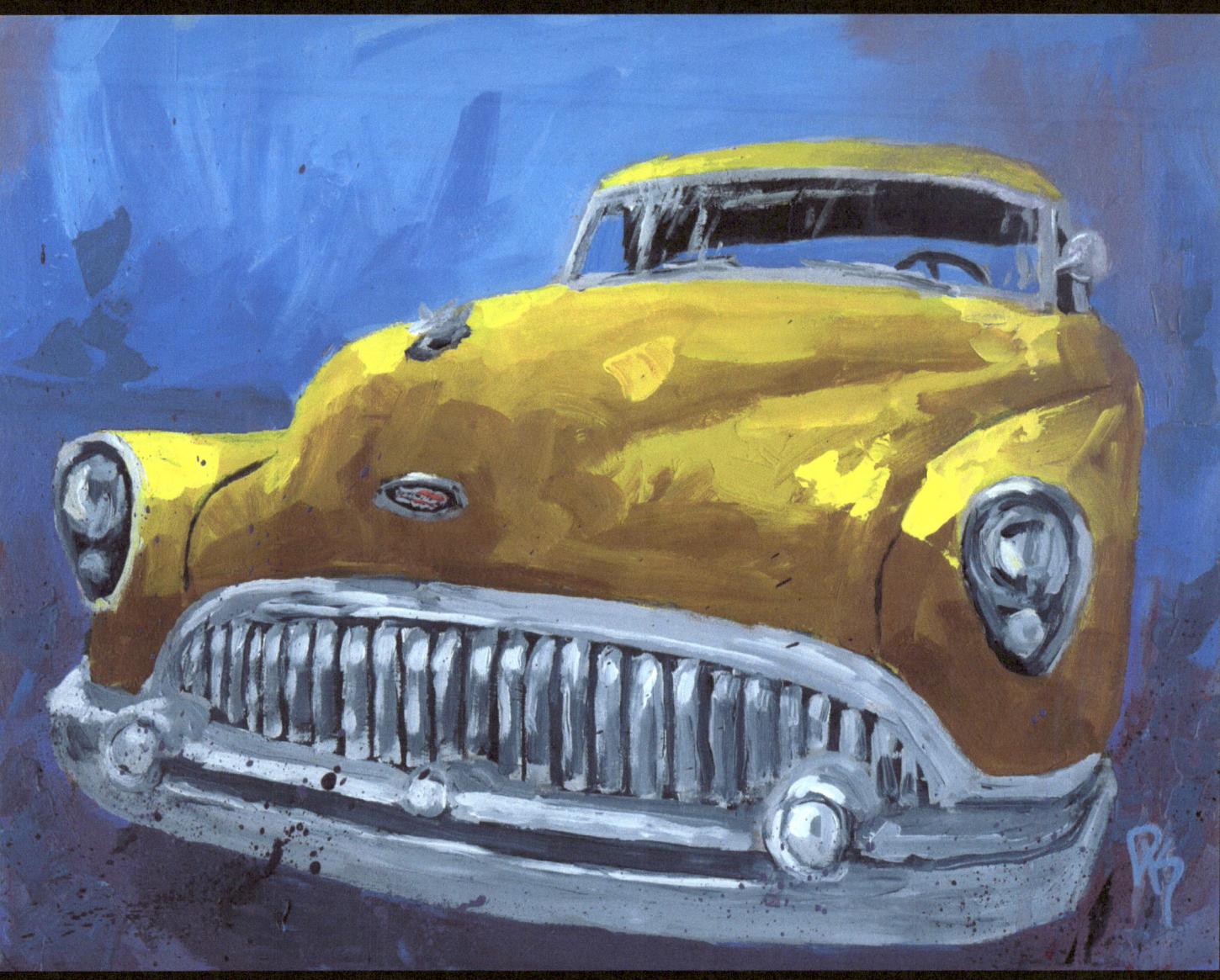

Purple Cadillac by David King Studio

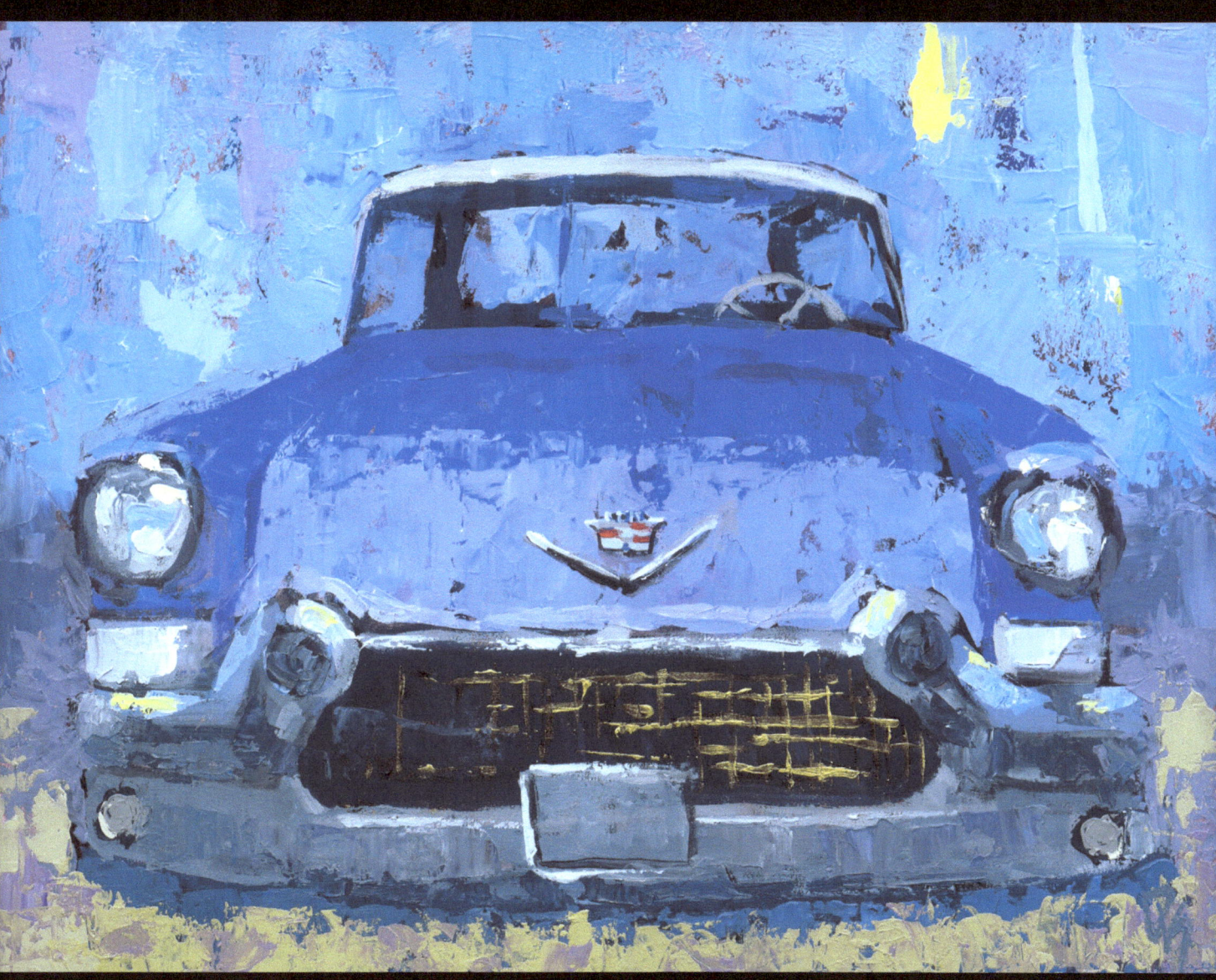

Green Beauty by Shan Peck

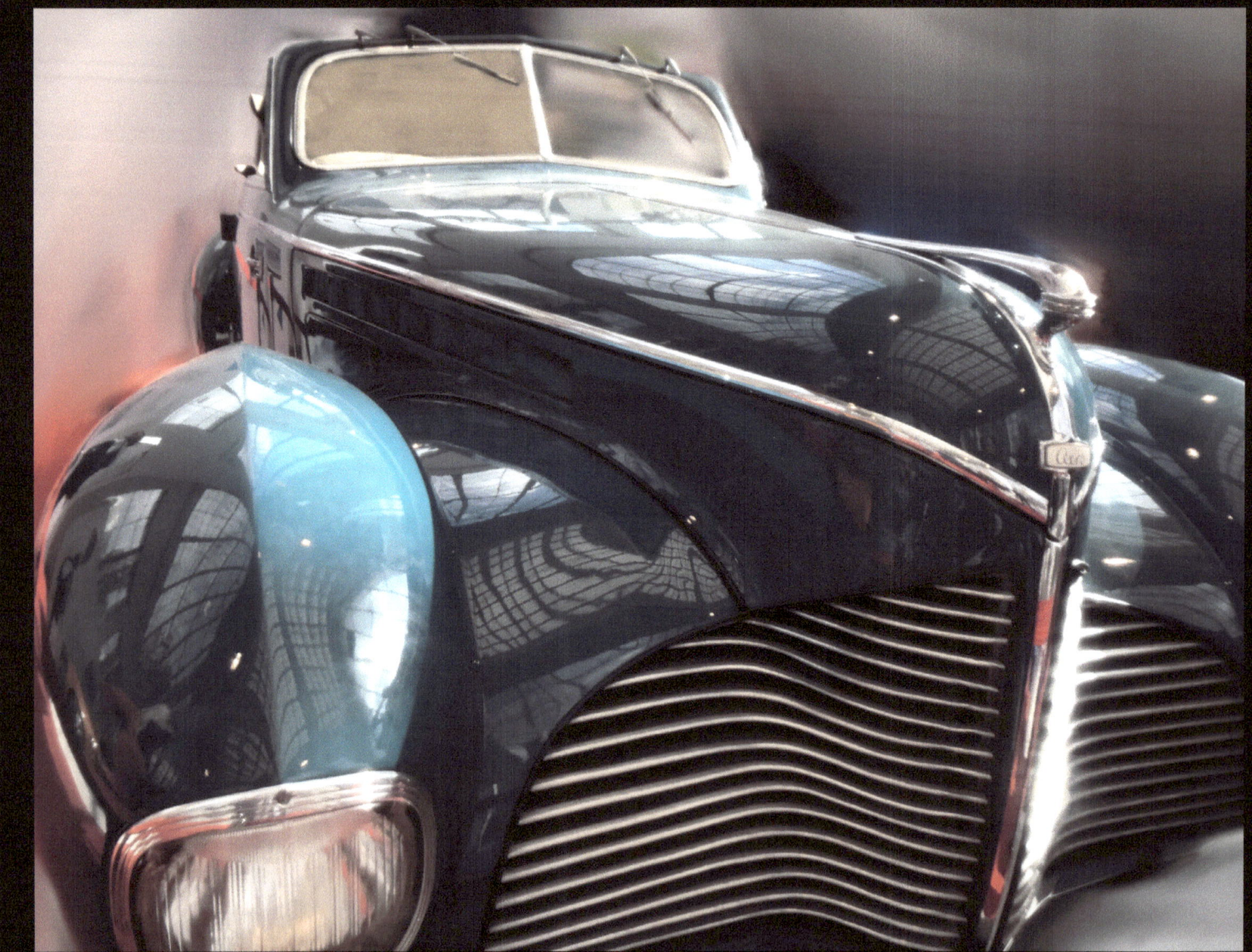

1950 Buick Roadmaster by Ron Patterson

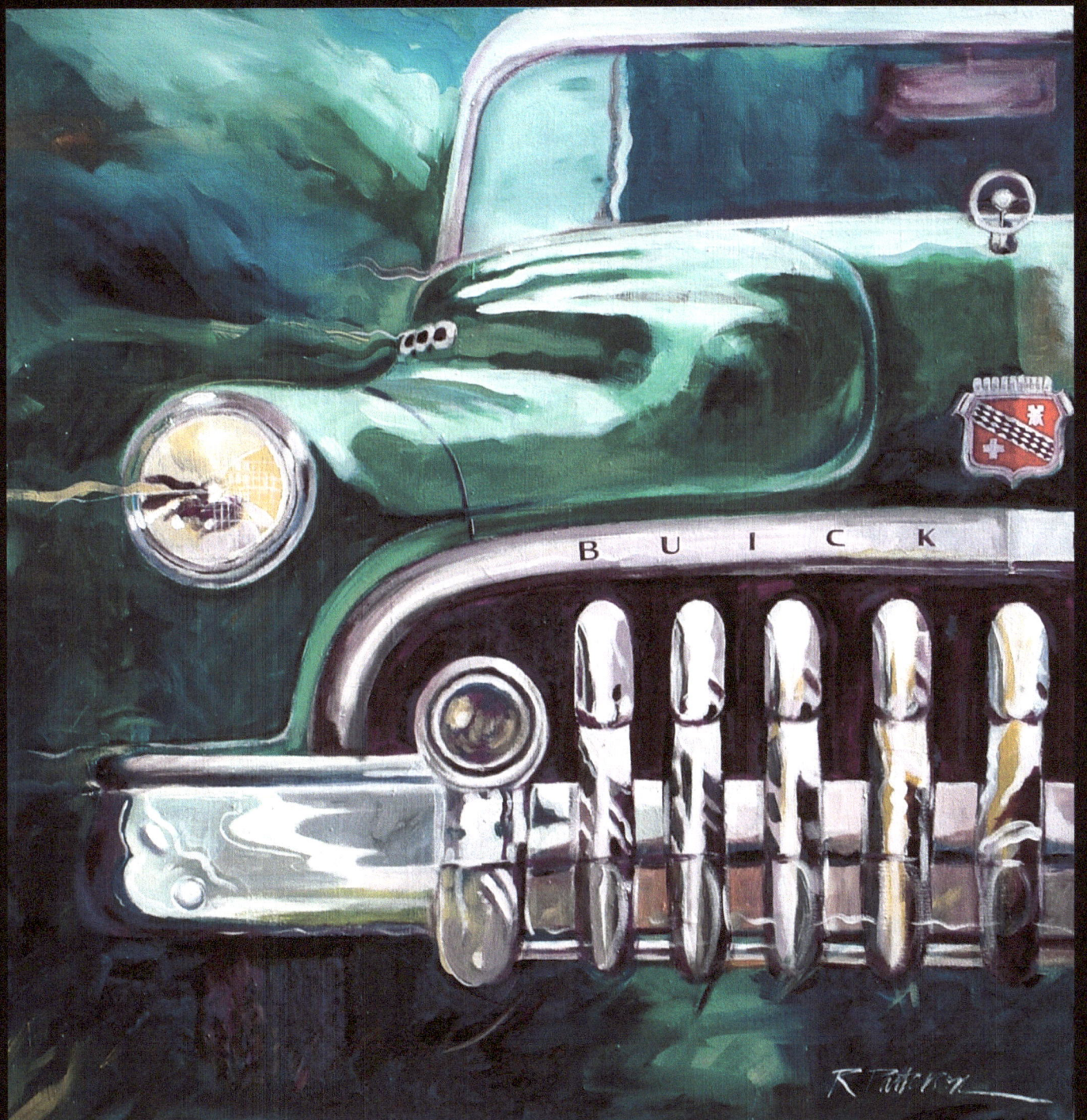

Tatra by Shan Peck

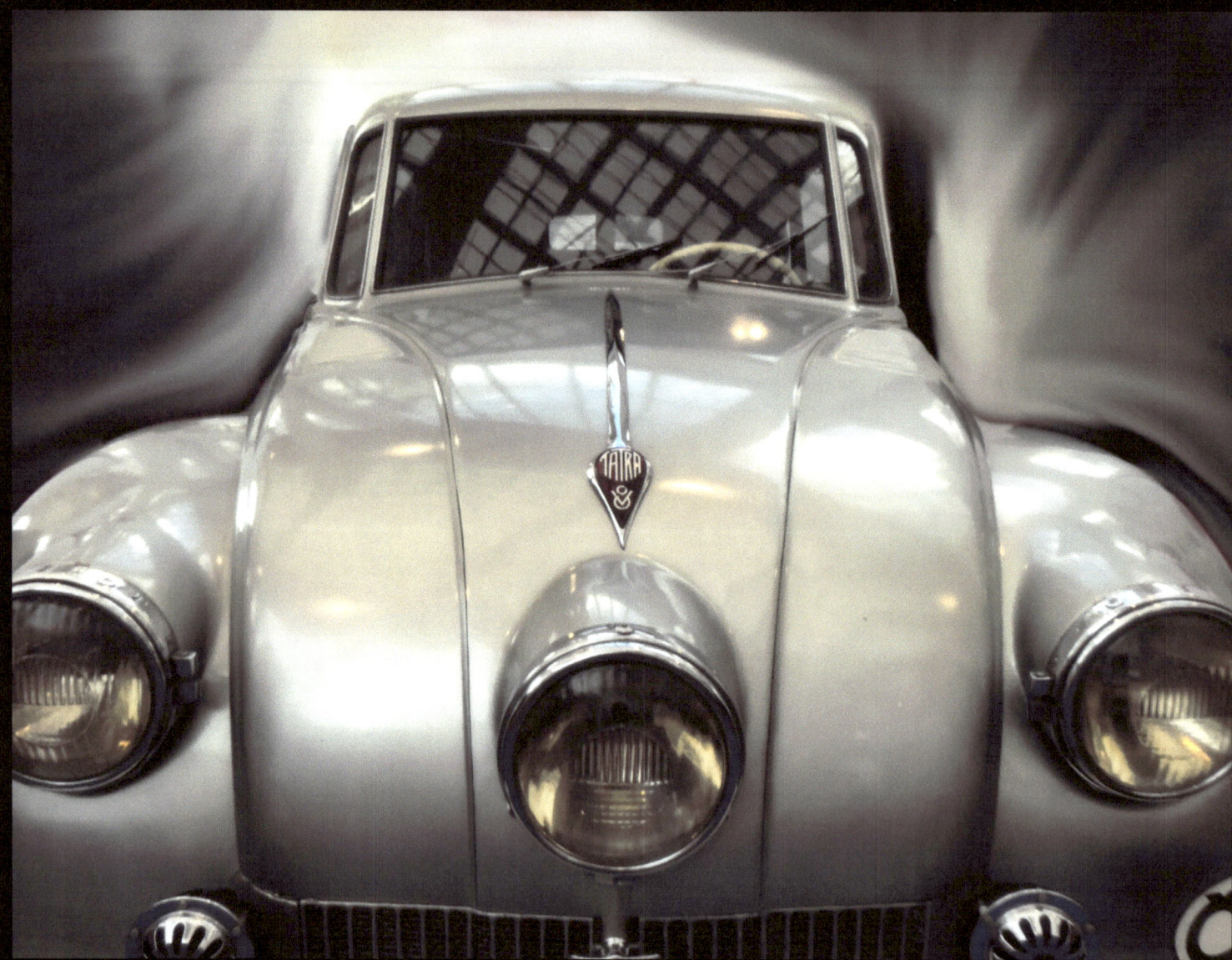

1951 Packard Clipper by Ron Patterson

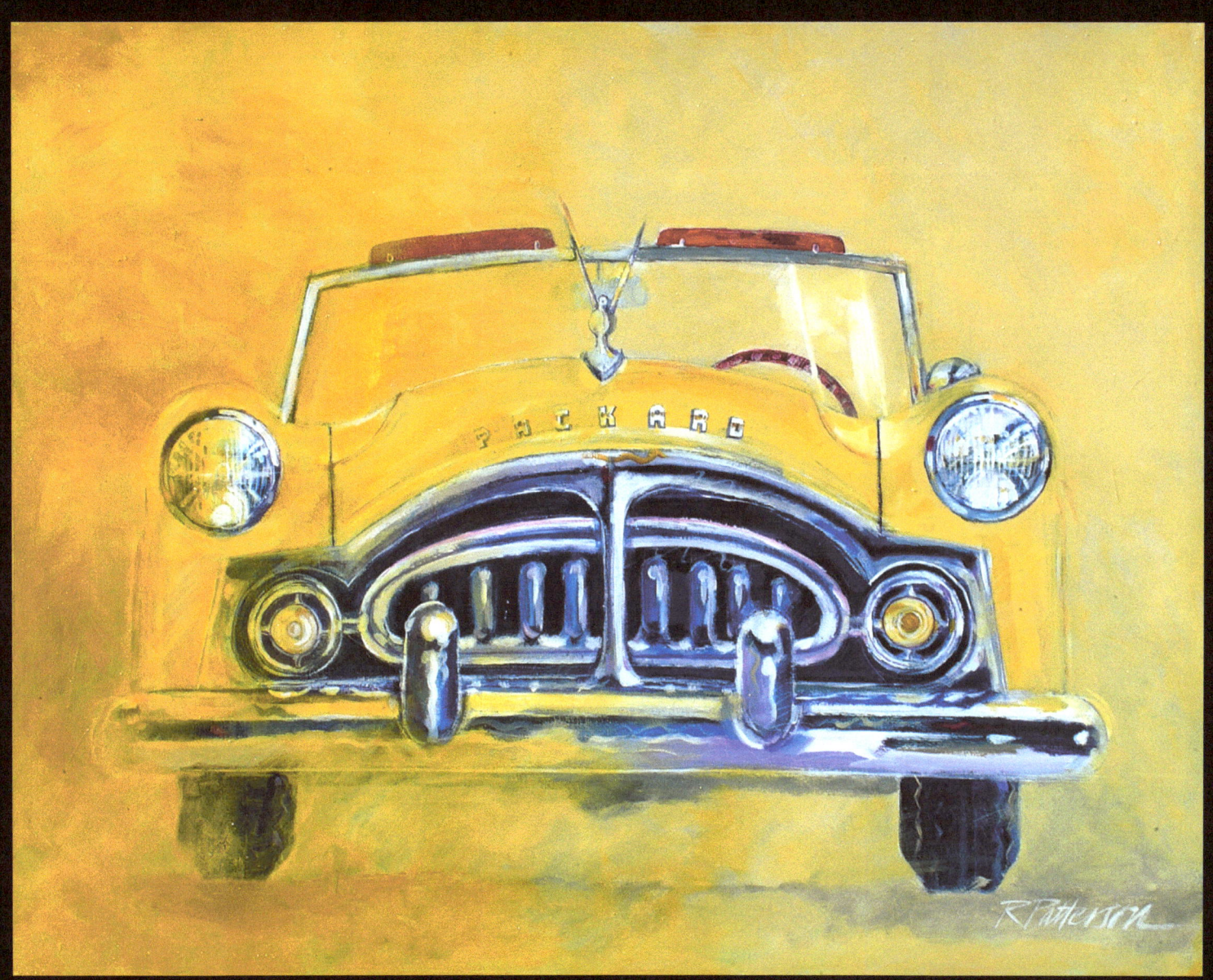

1949 Ford by Ron Patterson

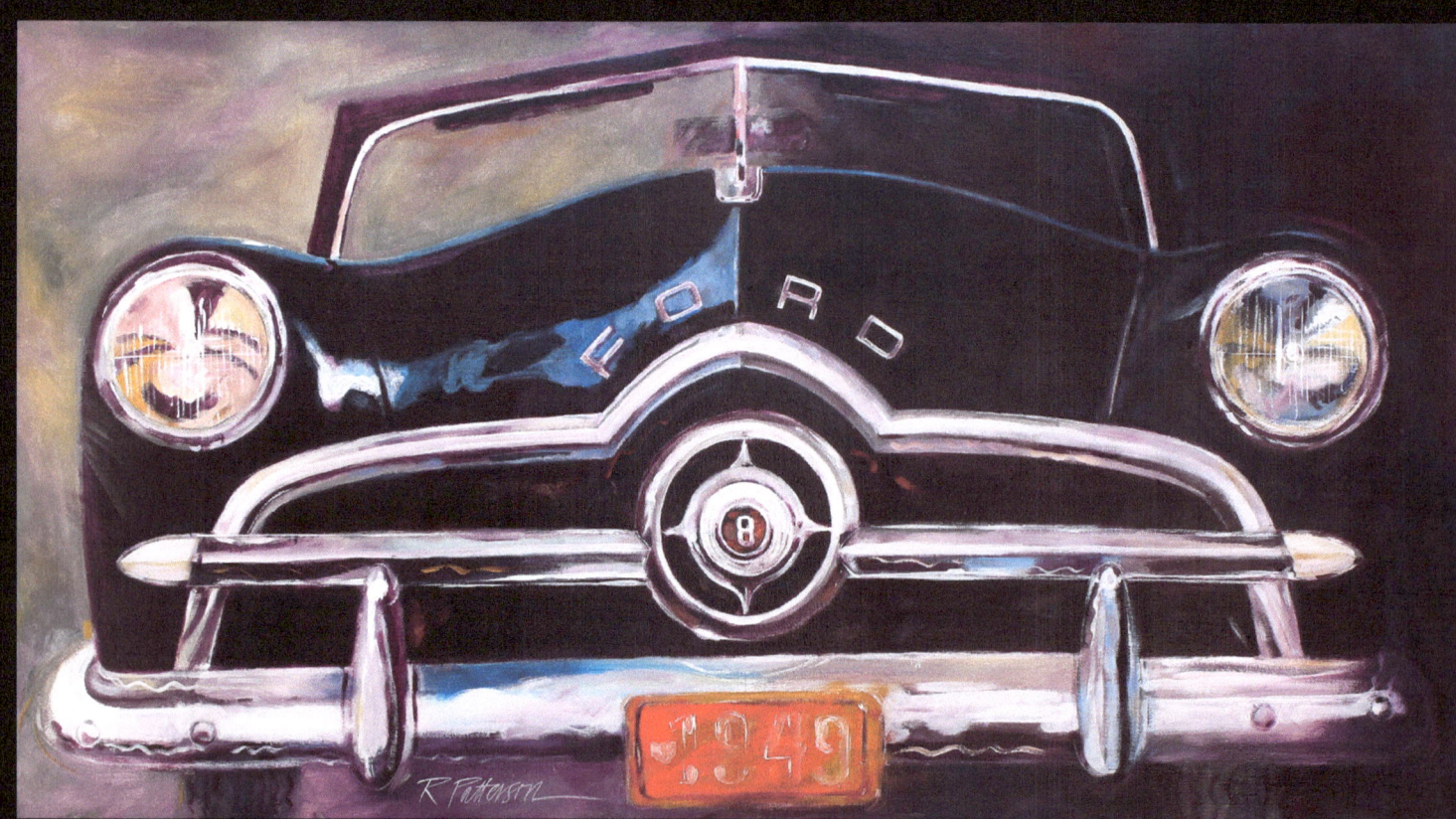

1951 Studebaker by Ron Patterson

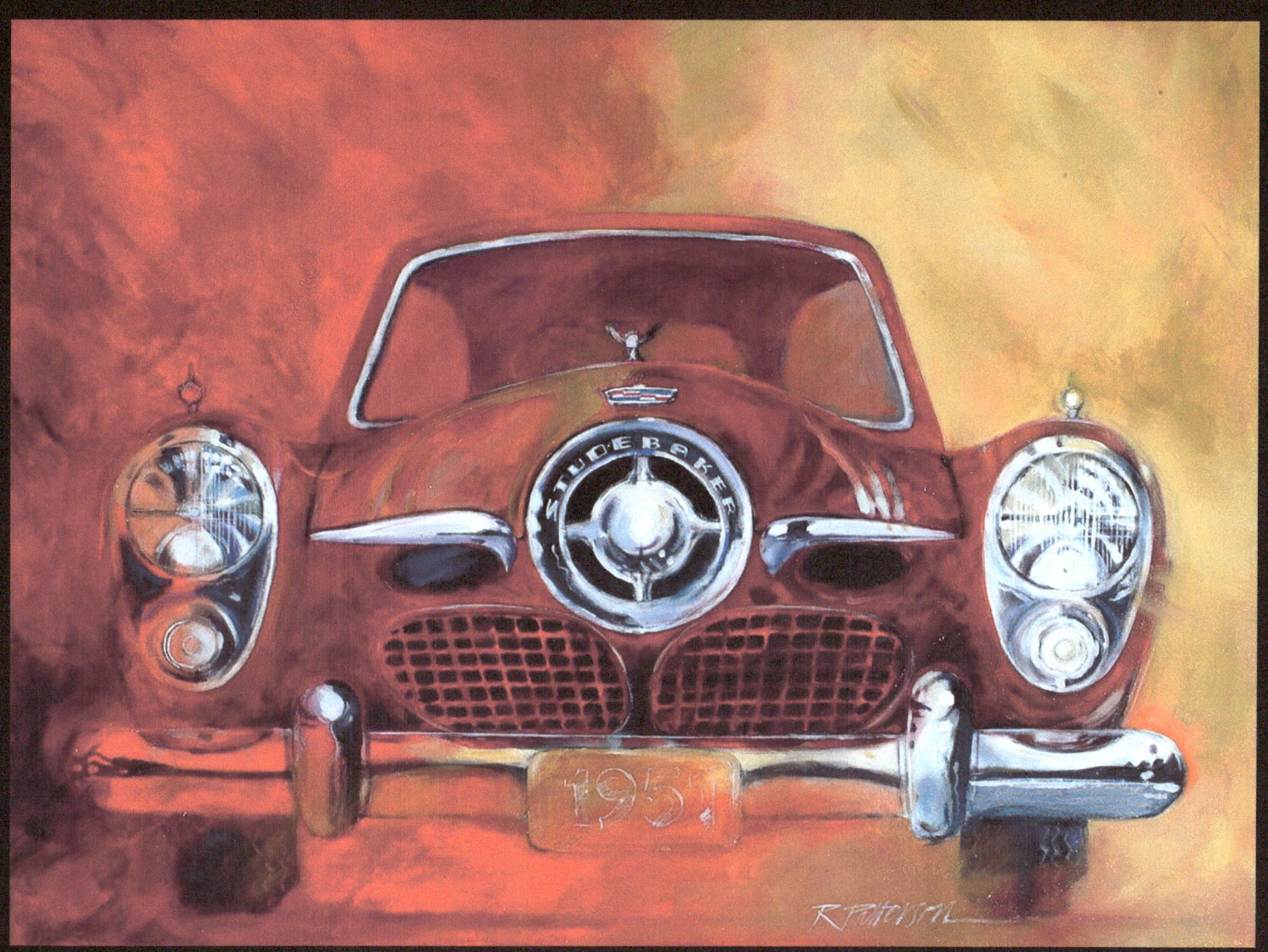

McArtor's Truck by Lance Wurst

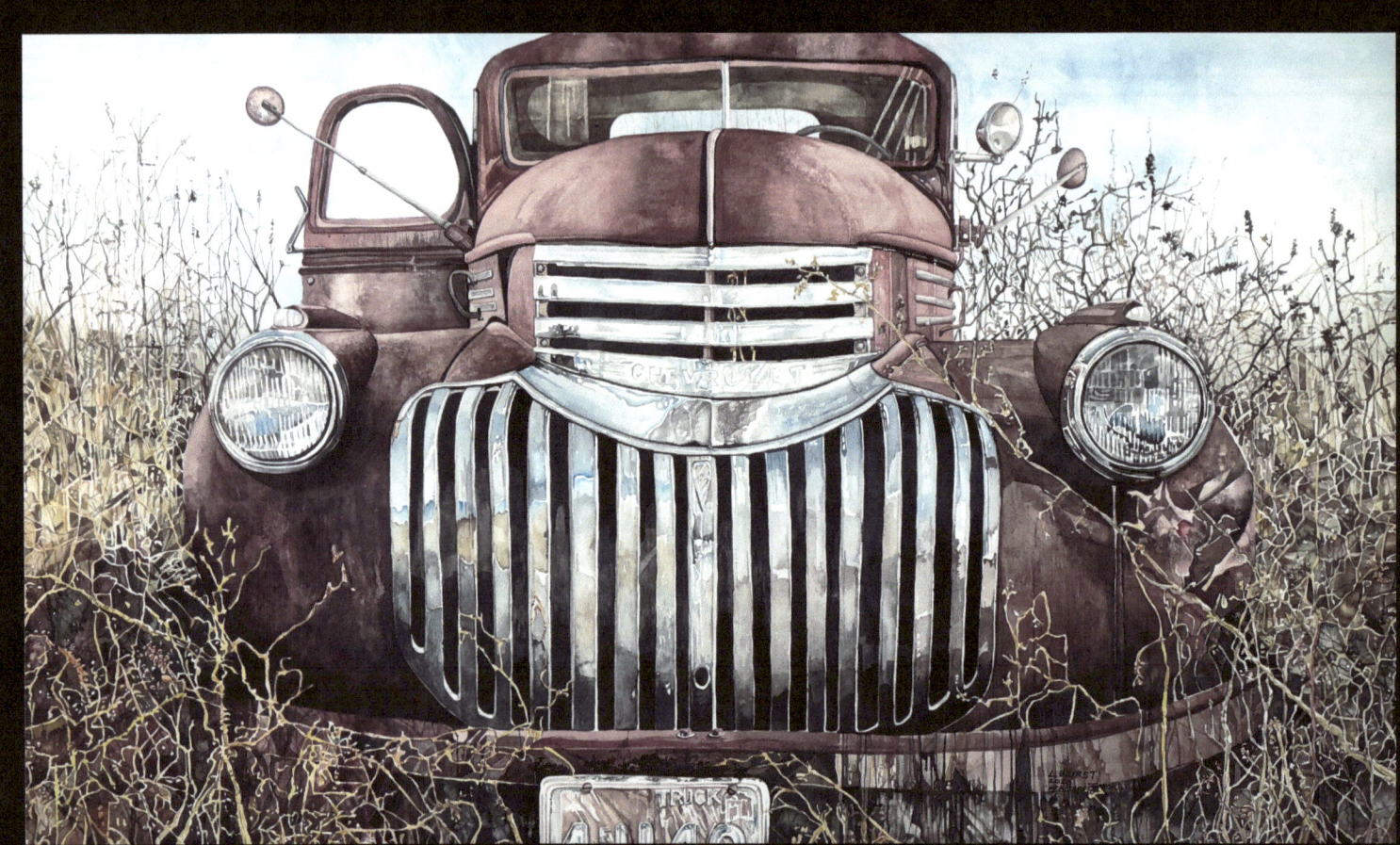

Chariot by Lance Wurst

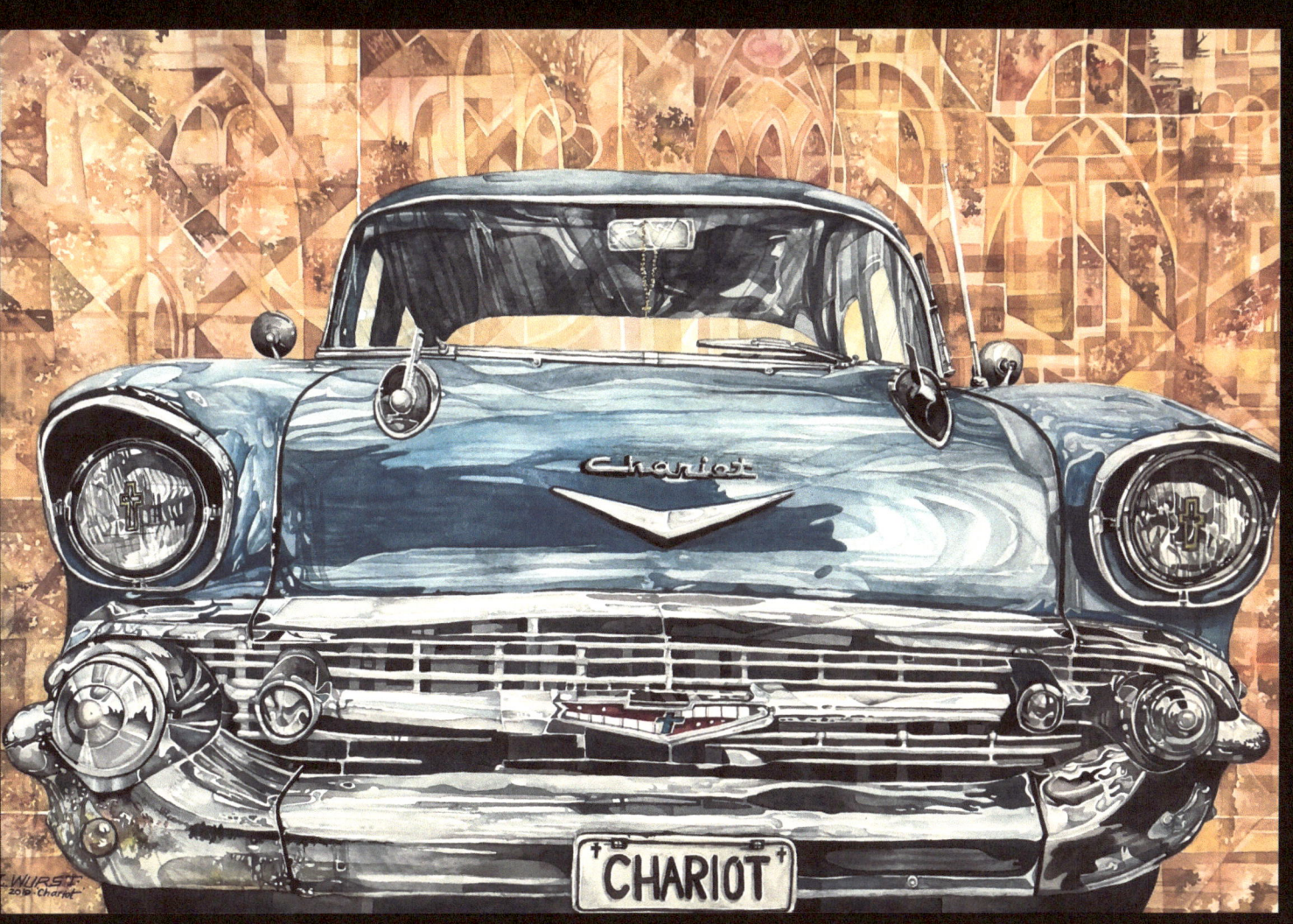

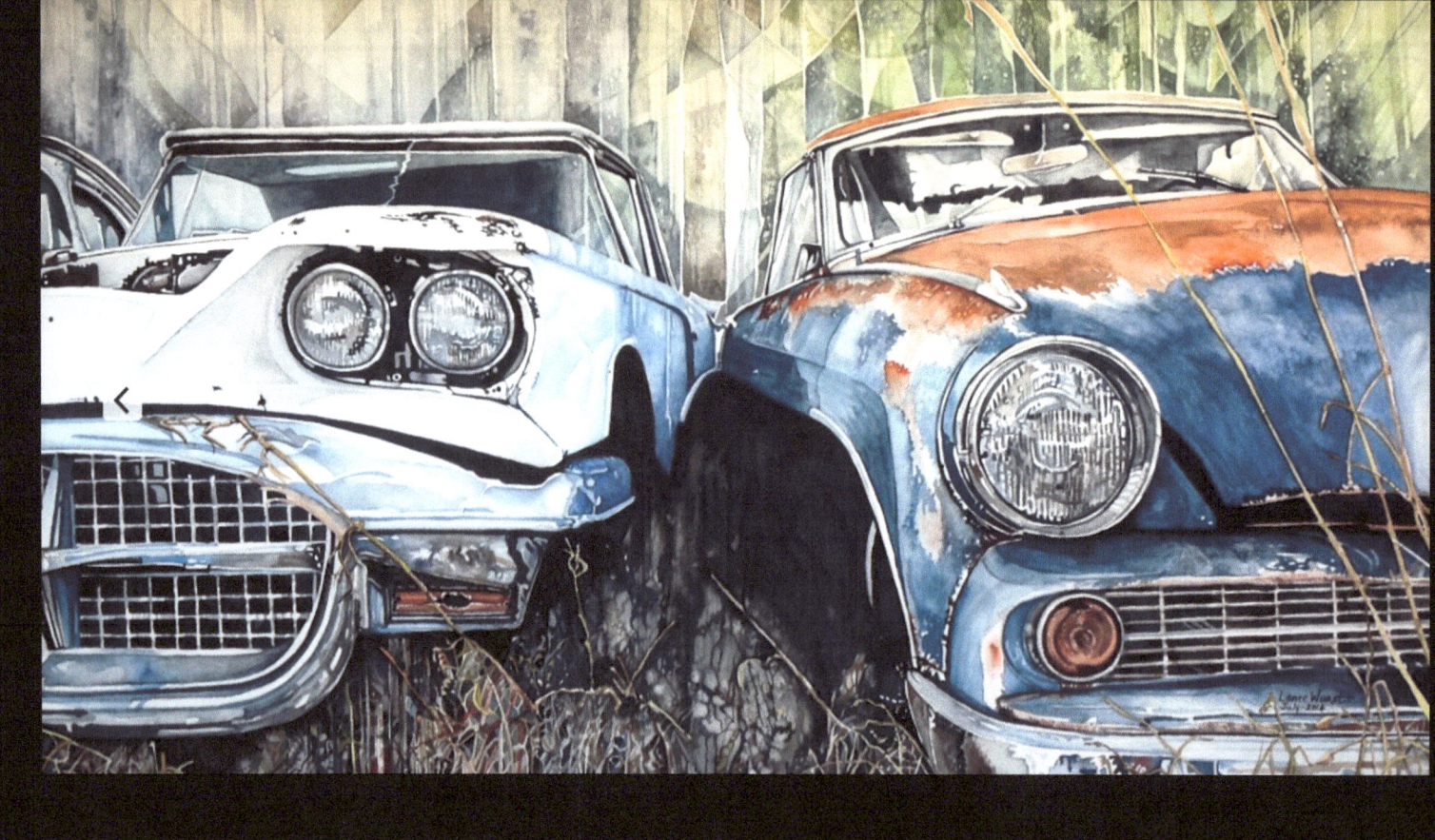

Sketch by Shan Peck

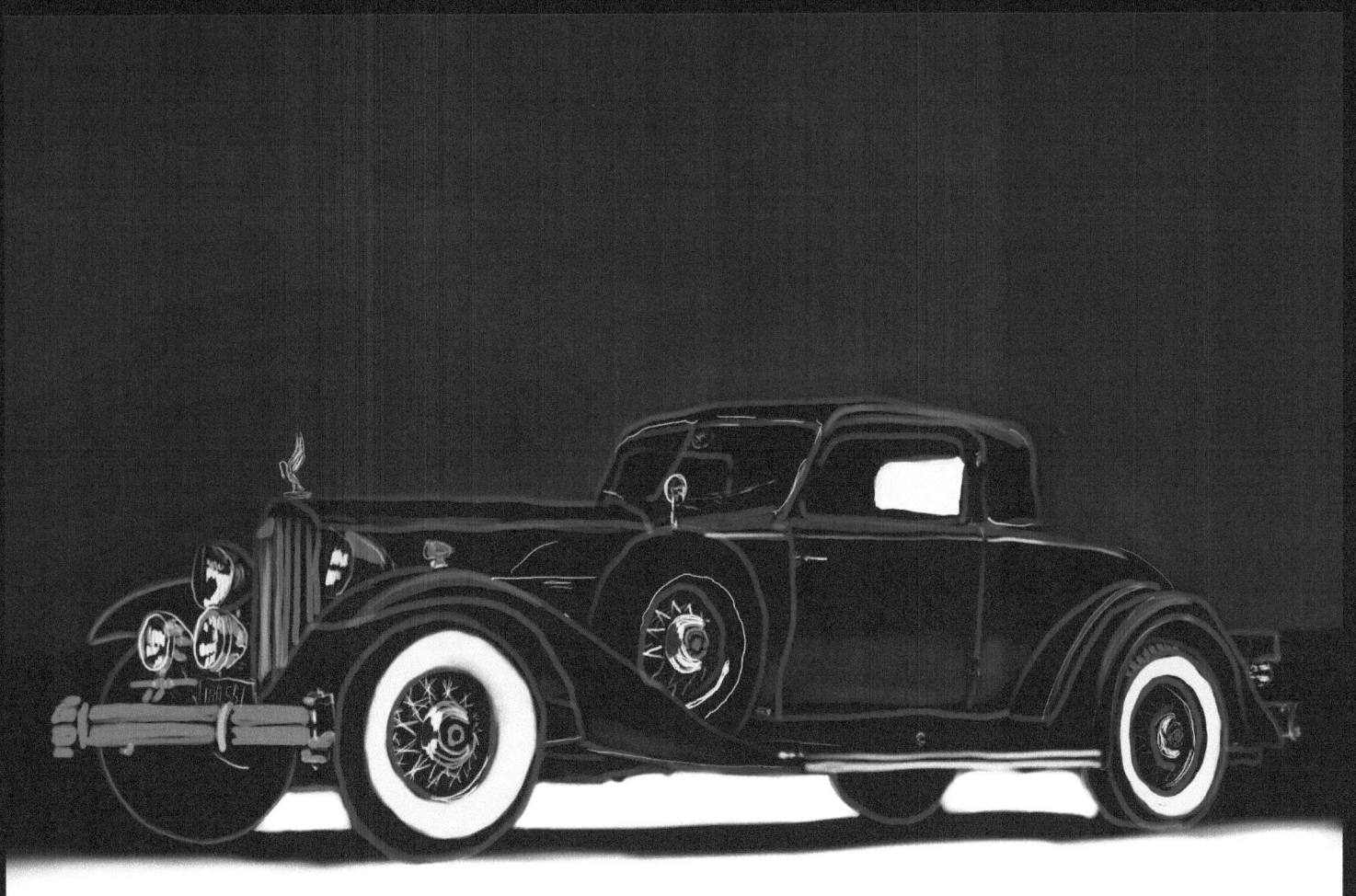

Summer Joy Ride by Shan Peck

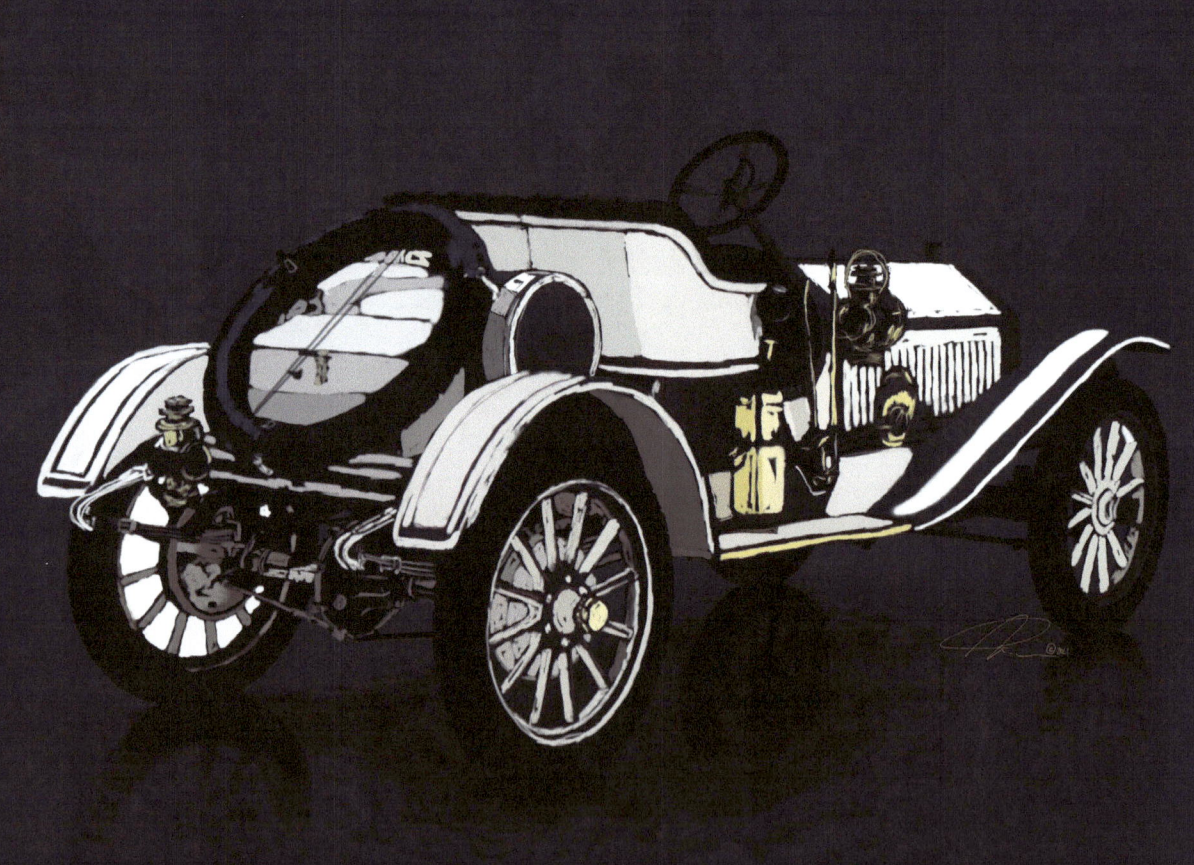

Earthquake Ready by Shan Peck

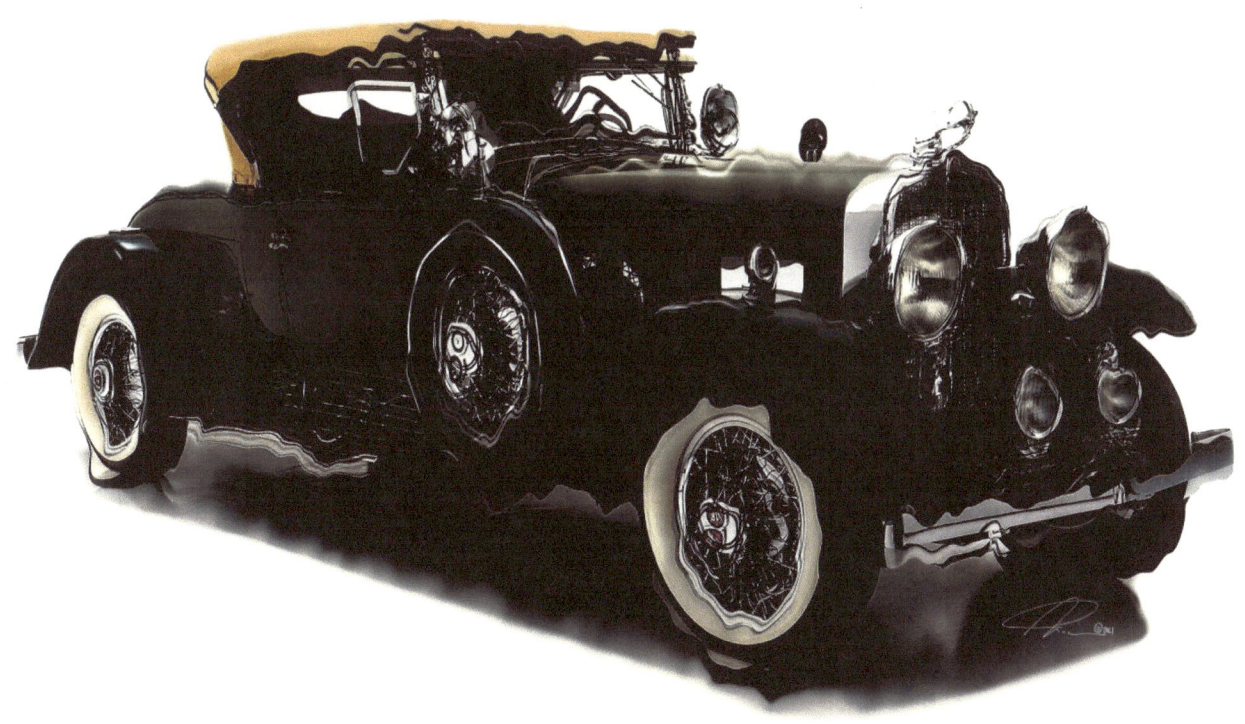

Sketch # Two by Shan Peck

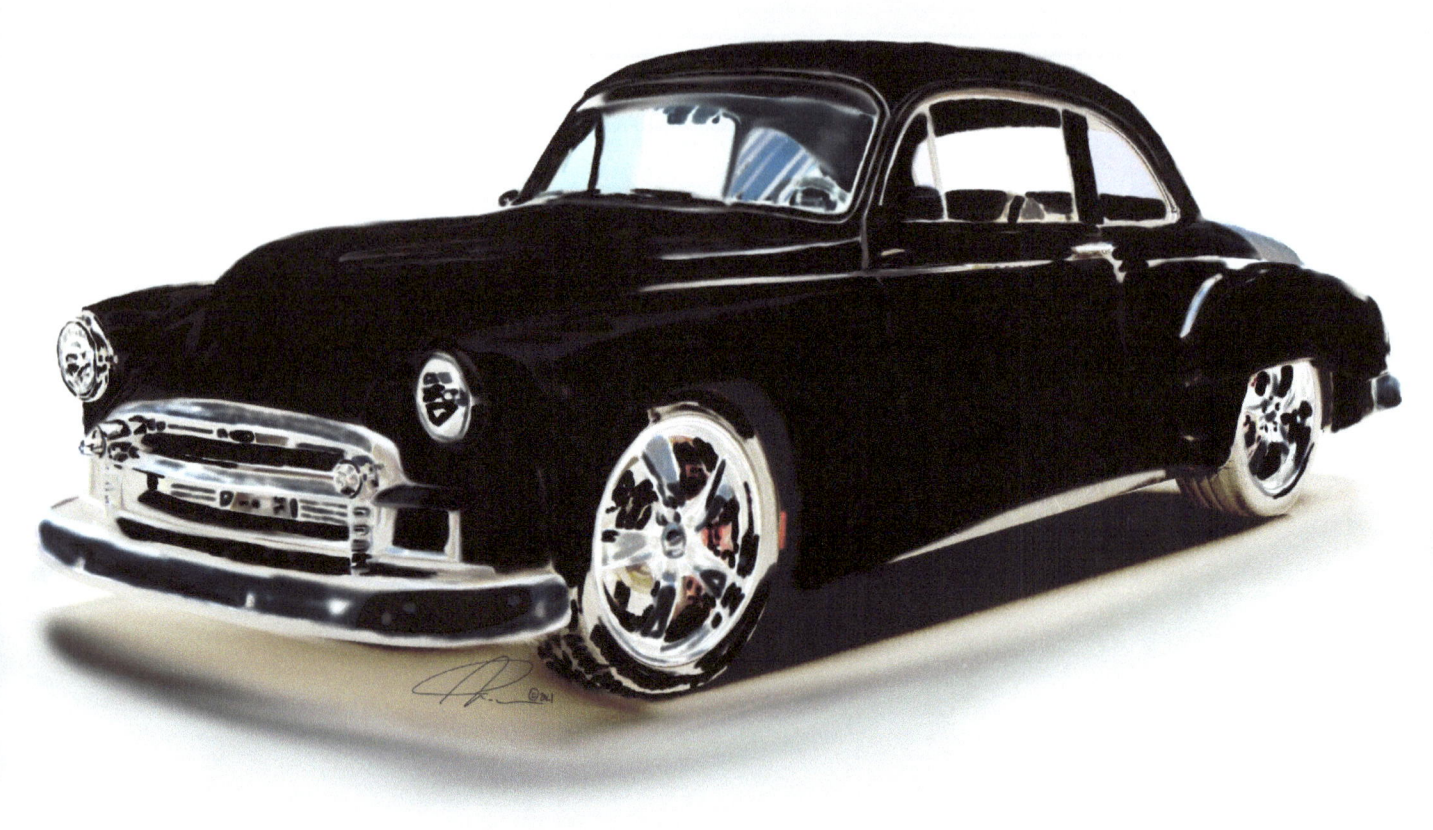

Pink Convertible by Shan Peck

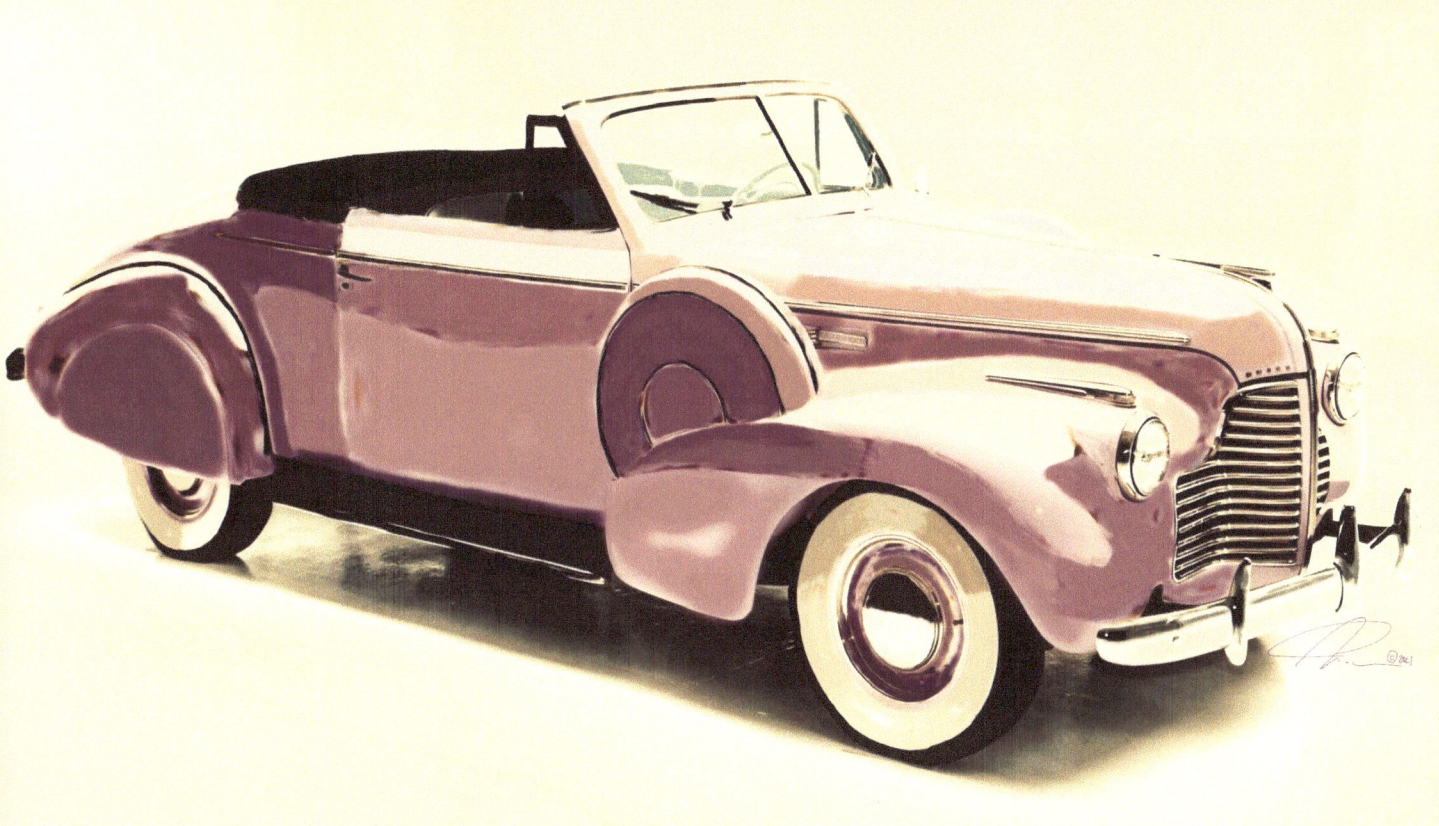

Color and Surface by
Shan Peck

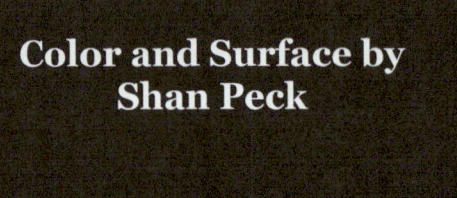

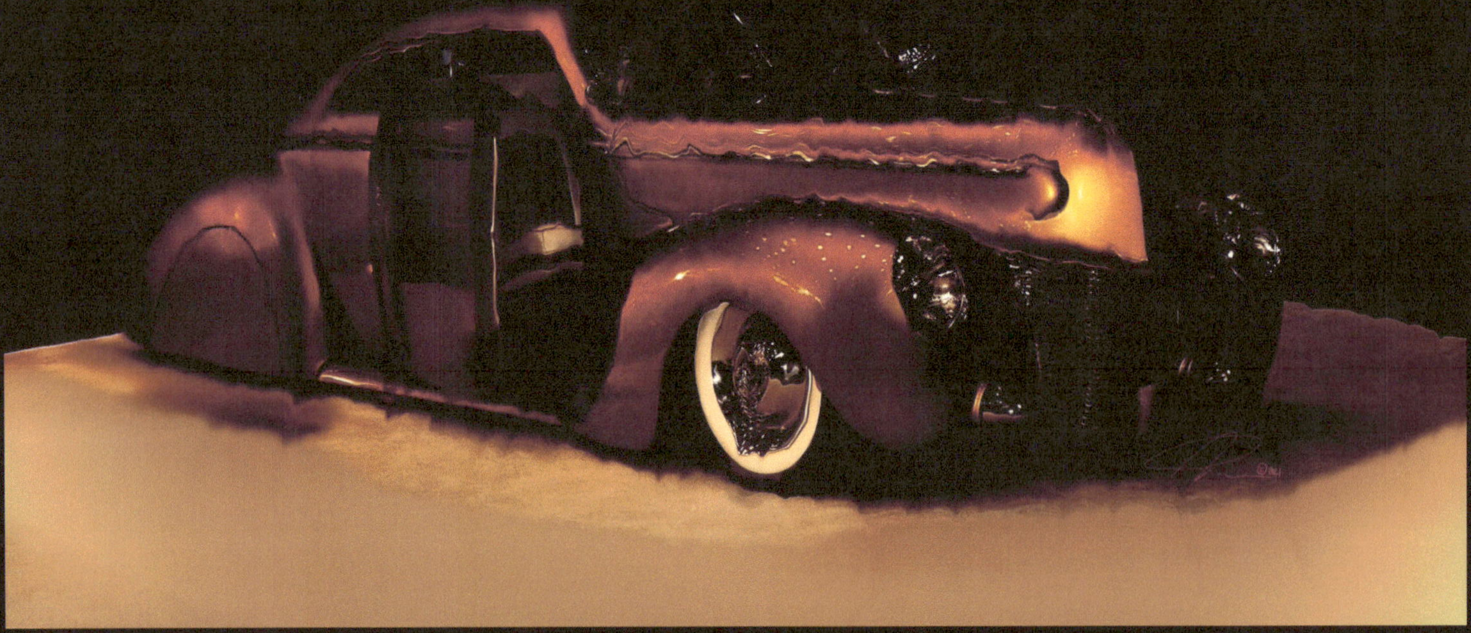

Selected Artists Email List

Lance Wurst - lrwurst@gmail.com

David King - davidkingstudio@gmail.com

Ron Patterson - ronp@rmi.net

ABOUT THE AUTHOR

At the age of 15, Shan Peck started to write short stories, poems, and screen plays. By age 19, he was working as a technician for film studios in special effects and lighting, and also worked on the movie, *Amadeus*, directed by Oscar-winning director, Milos Forman. At age 24, Shan emigrated to the United States and in 1989 he moved to California where he joined a Gilbert & Sullivan theatre group. While living in California, Shan attended Santa Barbara Community College where he took accredited courses in Business Law and Design. Following the death of his father in 2001, he returned to Czechoslovakia, his birth country, where he worked as a Quality Engineer, Quality Assurance Manager and Manufacturing Project Manager. While working in the automotive industry, he received Black Belt/6 Sigma training.

He has had several art shows in Europe and the United States and in addition to fine art painting, he has also done sculptures and spent significant time inventing technical and design improvements in fields like optics, acoustics and motion picture E2E2 systems. Shan is currently writing his second book, written in parallel as a screen play for the film.

E MAIL CONTACT: motyl_1999@yahoo.com
Follow me on Twitter at @shanpeck2011

www.ingramcontent.com/pod-product-compliance
Lightning Source LLC
Chambersburg PA
CBHW051821210526
45473CB00005B/1690